Postmortem Depression
And Other Maladies of English

Karen II,

thanks for all your
help during these
trying times. Hope
you enjoy this.

Jimmy

No Frills
<<<>>>
Buffalo
Buffalo, NY

Printed in the United States of America

Neureuther, Jimmy

Postmortem Depression/ Neureuther- 1st Edition

ISBN: 978-0-9910455-4-9

1. Postmortem Depression - Humor   2. New Author – No Frills.
3. Observation. 4. Life/Lifestyle
1. Title

No Frills Buffalo Press
119 Dorchester Road
Buffalo, NY 14213

For more information visit
Nofrillsbuffalo.com

This book is dedicated to Rick Malicki, who left us suddenly, October 10, 2009. We think about you often.

Postmortem
Depression
And Other Maladies of English

Compiled by Jimmy Neureuther

Foreword

The English language is one of the most difficult to master, even for those who speak it every day. There are words that sound the same but have different meanings. Sometimes we use several words to describe one thing. When words with completely different meanings have similar spellings, it's easy to get confused. Does John have a photogenic or photographic memory? Are you saving your money for prosperity or posterity?

This book is nothing more than a collection of mistakes, missayings and flubs that we all make in our daily use, or misuse, of our language. Mixed metaphors abound, as well as comments that might make you wonder what cocoon some of us grew up in.

I began noticing these things about four years ago. Some I heard directly, some I got second hand. I started keeping a note pad in my pocket and soon enough people knew they said something, when the pad and pen came out. I'm sure some thought I was a self-righteous jerk, poking fun at those who might not know they said something wrong. I've even received a couple comments to that point but I truly don't mean to offend anyone.

When you say, write or post something in public, and don't take the time to make sure it's correct, I consider it fair game. If you happen to find yourself in this book, and were caught unaware, please don't take umbrage. Consider yourself a rising star and by all means, keep up the good work. I urge you to buy a copy to refer to after you become famous.

I am currently collecting entries for a second book entitled, *This is My Piece of the Resistance*. I know there is a wealth of good material out there, so watch out!

My wife bought a new table for the hallway.
It has a slate marble top.
Half and half?

The past 40 years has been like a blink to my
eye.

Some people don't listen. You have to keep
going until they get it in their ears.
Maybe they can't hear you.

If we win this game, we're pretty much in
control of our own destination.
Most of us are.

You know what they say…ignorance is no
excuse for the law.
Yet they still use it.

Man, you really hit it on the nail.

I like to make my pasta el dante.

You should take Kinko Biloba. It might help
your Petula Oblongata.
I think you should take some.

Those kids really get my dandruff up.

The mind is a terrible thing.
Sure seems like it.

Don't get mad, I'm just yanking your crane.

She's only trying to shake your chain.

There's no ands, ifs or talking about it.

If you call after five p.m., you'll get their
animated help line.
Might make it more interesting.

We went to the notary public for our
honeymoon.
*You probably should have gone way before
the honeymoon.*

I've been working here long enough to know
that nothing is inevitable.
Some things are.

When my husband's grandfather died, he and
his brother were ball bearers.
Small casket?

That guy really nailed it on the head.
Of the nail?

It's as easy as fish on a hook.

I really don't want to do this. Guess I'll just
have to grid my loins.

I'll tell you, my husband made me so mad last night. I'm on my last rope with him.

When you put more wood on the fire, make sure you push it down into the ambers.

President William McKinley was assassinated in Buffalo, NY at the McKinley monument. *Talk about foresight!*

When it comes to money, some people are so fiberous.

It was just a spare of the moment decision.

You're in crouching on my side of the table. *Get off the table. There will be more room.*

You just wasted your time talking to him. It was all for not.

That knife had a serregated edge.

My brother's favorite snack is general salami. *How does the General feel about that?*

Don't worry. I'm sure calmer heads will prevail.
That's cool.

I'll bet those guys were making money hand over foot.

My neighbor said, "When you go to Mexico, you're expected to bicker with the street vendors."

My buddy married a very domineering woman. The whole first year he was walking on eggs.
Why did she make him do that?

Well, I guess it's back to ground one.
Is that anywhere near square zero?

They were busier than a pig in a sty.
How busy could they be?

I really don't want to drudge up the past.

John and I work well together because we're of the same mind thought.
Did you go to the same school set?

Remember all those great commercials from the '60s? My favorite was Pillsbury, the doughboy.
I never knew that was his name, or that he fought in W.W.1.

I just wanted to make sure he had all of his facilities.

My boss is always snapping the whip.
There seems to be a lot of bad bosses.

My brother is pretty good at playing pretend air guitar.
I'd like to see what he does with a real air guitar.

When we came around the corner, we were travelling at a high speed of rate.

What a beautiful girl. Her name escapes me right now, but it'll come to me when I think of it.
And not a second before.

That's in there so tight you'll need a wine cork to get it out.

How does it feel, now that the coin is on the other side?
I don't feel any different

If this works, we'll kill two stones with one shot.

Nothing beats a nice NY stirp steak.

That girl was so pretty all the guys went goo, goo, gaga over her.
That'll impress her.

You know how it is around here. Every time you turn around, it's another Saigon nonsense.

When it's muggy like this, it's harder to inhale and outhale.

I don't know why they do that, but I think
that's their method of madness.

That girl was miscombobulated.
I know her parents, Mr. and Mrs.
Combobulated.

That girl must be on a diet, or something.
She's twindling away to nothing.

We rented my favorite movie last night;
"Bridge Over the River Choir."

Sometimes the best way to learn a new job is
on hands training.

Last night I had a can of Dudley Moore beef
stew for dinner.
I wonder what he had.

We're too far from an electrical outlet. We
have to use an abstention cord.
You won't get any electricity with that.

After putting money in my 401K for three
years, I'm totally invested.

Lots of old castles had gargles along the top.

Things always seem to take longer when lawyers get involved. They all must have gone to the same school of technology.

This new timekeeping software is really a thorn in the company's aside.
Shh. Don't tell anyone else.

What do you mean, you don't understand? Are you trying to get artificial with me?
No! I don't understand for real.

I think you should tell your father about it, but don't let me twist your finger.
Go ahead!

Enter at your own risk.

It's not perfect, but it's good enough for my book.

If you need a pattern to follow, just take a piece of cardboard and make a tin plate.
Wouldn't it be a cardboard plate?

You know what they say… any porthole in the storm, right?
I've heard that.

My head would fall off if it weren't attached.
Yeah, I'm pretty sure mine would too.

Why don't you stick it where the moon don't shine.

Kool-Aid tastes better when you make it with dehydrated water.
It might taste better, but I'll bet it's not as wet.

This two by four feels awfully light. I wonder if it is made of Balsam wood.

He thinks he's king of the roost.
Does he also rule the hill?

It was a tragedy of the first proportion.

I don't care which way we turn. Half dozen or the other.

I swear, that guy is dumber than hammer shit.
He's not the only one.

They were really champing at the bit.

It smells like fromungous cheese.

He's got the short man simplex.
Sounds complex.

She didn't even cinch when I told her the bad news.

Everyone was googling and goggling to see the accident.

She's hard to understand because she has a speech impairment.

I kind of have a way to words.
I can see that.

The boss wanted me to put them in alphabetical order. You know, one, two, three, etc.

None of us is getting as young as we used to.
I don't ever remember getting younger.

That guy was as busy as a pig in shit.
No busier than if he was in a sty.

That guy doesn't know shit about shinola.
Neither do I.

If you need information about car repairs, you
can look it up in the Chitlins manual.
Auto repair and cooking in the same book.

For lunch, I had a calzone made with spinach
and regatta cheese.
Was it done el dante?

Would that be pronounced Buffoo?

I don't understand. Could you be more pacific?

The crook wore dark glasses because he wanted to remain incarnitos.

I don't understand why he got so disemboweled over the whole affair.

There was a big hub-hub at work today. It seems there might be a layoff.

I didn't mean to screech when I saw that spider. It was just a natural resource.
The spider or the screech?

With all that knowledge, I'll bet you're the boss's gopher guy.

His voice was raspy after the operation because they incubated him.
Might have been too hot in there.

Too bad we're not psychic. We could just use our mental palethany.
If we were psychic, we wouldn't have to use anything.

Looks good to me.

Some people just can't see the trees through the forest.
Wait until the wintertime.

I'm not going to worry about it any more. It's just water over the dam.
I'd worry.

Don't worry. I'm here till the duration.
But not after it starts.

I can see much better since I started wearing biofiles.

It's just another mountain in the middle of the isle.

The nightclub was chuck full of people, last night.
Chuck is a nightclub?

If my husband would have paid our bills, we wouldn't be in this ballpark.
Are you living there?

By the time I got there, they were already two sheets to the wind.
Guess you got there just in time.

Peter Sellers is my favorite comedic actor. I just love his portrayal of Inspector Trudeau.

I've got my ear on the pulse of that.

I have a real bad crink in my neck.

Don't come too close to me. I've got bronical pneumonia.

That guy's not the smartest tool in the shed.
Most of the tools I know are pretty dumb, too.

We went to see a musical, and sat up in the mezzaline.

You don't have to be a rocket genius to understand that.
I think you do.

I'm packing three boxes at the same time, but they're all twins.
That would be six, right?

For all intensive purposes.
Or any other purposes.

You can best avoid catching a cold by practicing vigorous hand washing.
Germs aren't very fast.

Those guys sure took an absorbitant amount of time to paint my house.
They wanted to make sure it all soaked in.

You have to be careful when working outside in the summertime. You could get heat frustration.
I hate when that happens.

When we walked into the kitchen, everything was a skewer.
Must have been difficult to eat anything.

My husband bought us tickets to see circus 'ole.
Is that the Spanish version?

It was way too much aggravation to go through all that rigor mortis.
I'd be pretty aggravated myself.

Those guys are like a bunch of cavemen.
Regular Cro-Magnums.
They'd be bigger, right?

Rod told me he was having trouble with his
prostrate gland.
*Couldn't get that sucker to stand up for
anything, huh?*

I hate having to deal with all that
rickamarack.

Most streets in the city have alternative
parking.

Don't say anything. You'll just be creating a
hornet's nest.
As long as you don't kick it.

Everyone knows you pay for what you get.

That plan will never see the day of light.

My dad has irritated bowel syndrome.

There is a special room at the casino, for the
big rollers.

I know you don't like the way those people
live, but that's just the color of the beast.

The mechanic said my car needs a new Cadillac convertor.
I would rather keep it as a Cadillac.

All this bad weather is caused by a storm system called El Meano.
A well deserved name.

I don't care about what those people say. I just let that stuff roll off my head.
That could be why they're talking about you.

When you fill out the application, you should use large case letters.

Come Monday morning, it will be back to the same old grindstone.
Do you work in a mill?

Those cars are different, but they look the same to the untried eye.
I tried. Couldn't tell the difference.

Be careful fighting this guy. He likes to go right for the jugs.
I've always thought women shouldn't fight anyway.

Ten minutes after he laid down, he was gone like a light.

For the last five years my cancer has been in remittance.
Where did you send it?

Some of the birds that fly at night? Owls, hawks, bats.

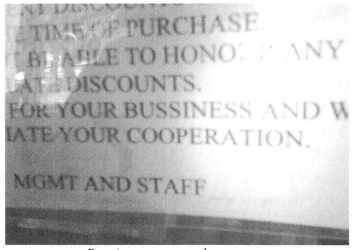

Bussiness as ussual

Those people are just giving you ear service.
I'll take care of my own ears, thank you.

They hummed and hawed over which
restaurant to choose.
*As long as you don't have to eat with skewers,
who cares?*

I feel like I'm in Nirvana.

I believe they jumped the ball this time.
At least they didn't drop the gun.

Welcome to my humble commode.

Michelangelo painted the ceiling of the
sixteen chapel.
Who painted one through fifteen?

Sometimes, life just throws wrenches at you.
Watch out for life.

That guy is as gay as a three-dollar bill.
I didn't know money had a preference.

Many older men suffer from premature
ejection.

I could easily read the notice on the wall,
because the lettering was bolded.

The new police captain rode rough shot over
his charges.

My brother was born with a disformed arm.

Don't you dare counterdict me.

…and the Lord said, "Let there be life."

Everyone knows hindsight is 50/50.
Didn't know that.

The company sent around a moratorium
dealing with safety.
What, no more safety?

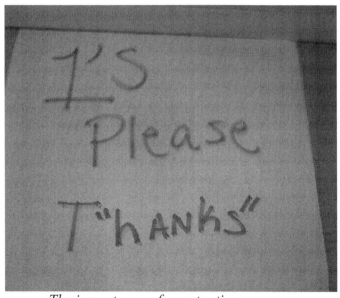

The importance of punctuation.

Don't ever forget; tomorrow is still here.
Will it still be here tomorrow?

Everyone knows the N.R.A. wheels a lot of power in Washington.

…and what am I? Chopped beef?
Is that better or worse than chopped liver?

We bought a new home, so we could be closer to my mother. Now she's just a skip, jump, and away.

I agree. That guy is smart, all right; smart like a rabbit.

You didn't have to tell the words right out of my mouth.

I shot that deer right in the neck. I think he bled out from the femoral artery.
I think you missed the neck.

All my life I've been fighting an uphill task.

I took a job with a company that is really service orientated.

You should see the level of compete that team has.

My wife went for her annual mammeogram. Next week she has an appointment with her GYS doctor.

Man, my boss is really on my neck today. *And he doesn't know why you don't get more done?*

Some of those guys are roofless. *I hope it doesn't rain.*

I like listening to him play his guitar with no accompliment.

Look at those wrinkles. I don't think the paint adhesed to the primer.

Let me tell you, around here they only want one thing or another.

I like Harvey Wallbangers. They're made with Vodka, Orange juice, and Galileo. *He's probably stale by now.*

I will need plenty of help with this project. I expect all of you to be on board the boat. *That's the kind of project I like.*

Beware the eyes of March.

We had our house covered in lunamin siding.

All right already, it's about time you got off your orange crate.

You can eat for free at the bar between three o clock and five. It's what they call happy time.
I would think so.

We'll take them to court. They don't have a foot to stand on.
As long as they don't have a leg, I think we're good.

For my new year's resolution, I'm dropping a new leaf.
I think I'm going to turn over a few bad habits.

I don't believe anything my boss tells me. He's always blowing sunshine up my ass.
I wouldn't believe him either.

We'll see what happens after all is set and done.

Getting married really put a crimp in my lifestyle.

I've always had that in the back of my head.
You should have it looked at.

Those guys do everything to the tenth degree.

Watching them win that game gave me
perspiration.
Was it audience participation?

That is so dusty, it must have been on the
shelf since the essence of time.

I watched a show last night that really perked
my interest.

I hate the way I look in that picture. I guess
I'm not very photographic.

My cousin remembers everything. I think he
has a photogenic memory.
I like the way it looks!

I still haven't cashed my paycheck from last
week. I guess I'm pretty spontaneous.

It was a tough battle, but with chemotherapy
and a little luck, her cancer went into
recession.

My cousin's wife had a hard time getting
pregnant, so she got herself artificially
assimilated.
Into what?

I know my user name and password are correct. I'm thinking that there's a glintch in the system.

Don: Can you name any of the three words in the English language that begin with dw?
Bob: D.W.I.

That guy's a big liar. He's got more crap than Carter.
They make a pill for that.

A young woman had to drink a chalky liquid before her M.R.I. She told the nurse she was going to try to imagine it tasting like her favorite drink; a metropolitan.

When we found out our mother was alive, it was like a brick was lifted off us. Before that point, we were just reaching for straws.

What a mess! This room looks like a whirlwind.
Don't let it hit anything.

This reminds me of an episode on "Tales From the Crib."

Man, I hate those people to a passion.

'Nuff said.

I put them just outside the door. I'm sure if you go look again, it will be pretty obnoxious where they are.
That's your fault, not mine.

My car has only a four-cylinder engine, but it has pretty good exhilaration.

Money is the route to all evil.
Go a different way.

After her baby was born, Debbie experienced a bad case of post-mortem depression.
How could she tell?

We devised an experiment for testing our hypotenuse.

You can't let this go too far. You have to nip it in the butt.

I don't know why I'm so lucky; I must have a four-leaf clover on my back.
Got to be more comfortable than a horseshoe up your ass.

My Aunt and Uncle are devote Catholics.

My wife went to bed early last night. She said she was feeling a little under the wind.

If you could buy anything you wanted, what would it be; assuming money is no option.
How would I pay for it?

I'm turning a new leaf.
Just don't drop it.

Careful, if you get too close you might put yourself in intimate danger.
I'll keep my distance.

I believe they ran the entire gambit.

Oh my God. There's a geico on my window.

There have been a lot of complaints lately, and our department is getting the blunt of them.
As long as we don't get the sharp ones.

I didn't realize you were talking to me. I thought I heard you out of the corner of my ear.
Maybe you need some ear service.

Every year around this time, we hear merchants complaining that holiday sales are not what they were expecting. Oh well, wake up and smell the roses.
That's right. Life isn't always a bed of coffee.

My car has a large engine. You would have to be an extortionist to reach a couple of the spark plugs.
I wonder what he would charge for a tune up?

In an advertisement in the want ads…
Carpenters wanted. Pay commencement with experience.

Cable TV is pretty much the same as pay for view.

I know the candidate won the popular vote, but didn't get very many electrical votes.
Maybe that state still has write in votes.

Behind the line of trucks was a single truck. I don't think he was part of the carrion.

My wife suffers from clusterphobia.
I don't care for them damn clusters either!

The switch is broken, but I think I can fandango something temporarily.

My neighbor has a huge dog. I think it's a rock wilder.

My husband always holds the door for me. I guess shivery isn't dead after all.
Close the damn door.

You really don't have to be a brainstorm to figure that one out.

The unruly prisoner was sent to solidarity confinement.

Sure they did something wrong, but never got in any trouble, all because they were burro cats.

You never use your tools any more. Are you saving them for prosperity?

I will read mysteries, drama, comedies; I like all genders.
Didn't need to know that.

I read an article that said Thyroid disease was quite prominent in Western NY.

The next new car that I buy will have all the bells and horns.

During a job interview, a young woman was asked, "Tell me about something that frustrates you." Without batting an eye, she said, "When my husband hits me."

The F.B.I. had an information leak. They believed they had a mold in the office.

My Russian uncle said he used to be an agent for the KGG.

If my boss gives me trouble about being late, I'll report him to personal.

My daughter-in-law brought home a new puppy. It was a Lavador retriever.

You really have to give people clear and decisive instructions.

Everything at the fair is three dollars, so bring
your three-dollar bills.
The gay ones?

Yes, those are still available. I just ordered
one off-line.

People will always remember you; you're like
a hallmark envelope.
Someone must have forgotten the card.

You know what they say; when the rat's
away, the mice will play.
They say that too?

I don't know what that is either. Your guess is
the same as mine.
And just as good too.

Nobody at work cared for that guy. They
treated him like a piranha at the office.
I can understand that.

I sent my money via wire transfer on Friday,
but the bank never got it. Now my money is
stuck in lingo until Monday morning.

He went to bed drunk and must have died
during the night. When we found him he was
stiff as a brick.

Some of the animals in this exhibit are a
species of themselves.

No matter what you say, you can't lie your
way out of this one. The surf's up.
Watch me hang ten.

We weren't sure what color to paint the
bedroom, so we went to the paint store and
picked up some color swabs.

The band had to stop playing by ten thirty
because our town has a noise orderance.

Don't give me all that useless information.
All I need to know is what's the bottom of the
story.

The woman said that men always touched her
rear end because it was the most assessable
part of her body.
They were only assessing it.

I finally received my abadand from my
lawyer.

Is that past tense?

I'm having a new minoleum floor installed in the kitchen.

My neighbor is 84 years old, and still quite thirsty.
Maybe she should stop being so feisty.

At the end of every rainbow is a silver lining.
So, the gold is now in a cloud?

She woke up late, and was nostalgic for the rest of the day.
Maybe she should go back to bed.

My doctor told me I have a high natal hernia.

My wife's brother was born with a congenial
heart murmur.
At least he didn't have a nasty one.

That's certainly a load after my mind.
It's ok, as long as it stays off it.

It's the same old horse and pony show, if you
ask me.
I won't ask.

My daughter really knows how to pull my
buttons.
She's just making up for pushing them earlier.

My mother was a very arid reader.
*Good thing. Books don't do very well in
water.*

The new guy has been on the job about eight
months, but he's still a little green behind the
ears.
Maybe some vigorous washing?

I didn't want to say anything. That's all I
needed to do was open another bag of worms.

Come on, we're going to be late. Chip chip.

Celiac disease is very popular in England.
That may be, but I don't know anyone over here that likes it.

My neighbor has been working for the police department for ions.
Ions don't pay the bills.

I haven't read much lately. I'm having trouble getting used to my bipolar lenses.
Gotta catch 'em on a good day.

As long as she's working, she's as happy as a clam in shit.
That's quite busy, too.

That guy doesn't know his ass from a hole in the wall.

Everyone knows it takes two to tangle.
It would be hard to tangle with one.

There is only one way to get there, and that's by boat or plane.

He'll never believe you. It's hard to pull the blanket over his head.

My mother always told me to do onto others, as I would have others do onto me.

Those guys are always getting into trouble. I
guess they don't think the rules occur to them.
I'll bet they don't.

He went through that money so fast, you'd
think it was burning a hole in his fingers.

We had good seats for the show. We sat in the
second row from the first row.

I couldn't believe it when I heard what you
did. I was upraged.
I know. I could hear the outroar.

I just don't know what to do. I feel like I'm
stuck between the devil and a hard place.
*That's better than being between a rock and
the deep, blue sea.*

It's just like I was telling… somebody.

It always helps if you've got friends in places.

He did more damage than a bull in a china
cabinet.
Must have been one hell of a cabinet.

Where were you all night? You look like
death worn over.
Worn over what?

The government doesn't care about us. This time they really sold us out to dry.

My all time favorite actor is Marlo Brandon.

What causes the grass to get mildew on it every morning?
Must be some moisture somewhere.

We were at the club last night and they allowed us to go up into the P.I.P. section.

Sometimes things just don't work out the way you expect them to. It's not always stars in heaven.

It's hard to believe that you people can't think past your heads.
I don't believe it either.

I don't like the thought of being at someone's beckoning call.

I had a will made but I'm not telling you any details until I'm dead.

Don't let that leak in your roof go for too long, or you'll have another can of problems.

John must not have gotten his raise. I just saw him walking in the hall with his tail between his ass.

That was just another one of his scatter schemed ideas.

Mexico's day of independence is celebrated on Cinco de Minco.

If you really want to lose weight, you need to do something to curve your appetite.

The only way you'll ever get those keys is under my dead body.

That did it! Now I'm really at the end of my straw.
It's not your last one, is it?

I liked his speech until he came up with a couple off the top comments.
He does tend to go over the wall at times.

I have a very basic understanding of sign language from working with death people.

I think that was a bad investment. You're just pissing good money after bad.

Yes, I know who he is. I've had the treasure
of his company.

Things were going just fine, and then they had
to drop that bombshell on us.
Was she a blond? Did any one get hurt?

I remember when that place used to be
nothing but a little hole in the ground.
*I think I know someone who wouldn't know
the difference.*

We were hungry so we stopped at this little
mom and dad restaurant on the way home.

I just made it by the skin of my back.

We don't see that happen very much. In fact,
it's an ararity.

We're going to have to cipher some gas out of
your tank.
2+2=4. 6x3=18. Got any yet?

Where do you stand on the subject of tart
reform?
I like them the way they are.

I'm so broke I don't even have two nickels.

Everyone knows you can't get milk from a rock.
Has anyone ever tried?

You can't do anything about it now. It's past the statue of limitations.

Well, what's done is done, but someday I'll see how it is on the other side of the grass.

He seemed to be in fairly good health and then one day he just hit the bucket.
I wouldn't worry unless he kicks it.

I don't know what to think. That's sort of a black area.
Not as vague as a gray one.

I was sitting around and that thought just popped into my hair.

I don't know why he got so mad. It was all out of good fun.

I took a walk in the woods and got burlaps all over my pants.

Sorry, I wasn't paying attention. I've really got a lot on my head lately.
It's not that commercial, is it?

My sister told me she once had an outer body experience.
I once had an inner one.

Man, were we lucky. We barely made it by the skin of our asses.
You were lucky! Back skin is a lot thinner.

All the stuff left after the garage sale was free for the getting.

That's not the worst of it. You haven't heard the top of the story yet.

We weren't able to get tickets to the game, but we can probably buy some from a scalpel.

You kids can wander around if you want, but make sure you stay within eyeshot.

I'm so broke I don't even have a penny to piss on.
You should have saved all those pennies.

I think I'm coming down with a cold. My nose is running like a bandit.

It all happened so fast. That deer ran out and I hit it. My airbag was employed in seconds.
I wish I could find a job that quickly.

There is a good horror movie on tonight, but if that's not your bag of tea, we can watch something else.

Wasn't it, though?

My uncle has a lifetime prescription for Playboy magazine.
There's nothing like naked women for what ails you.

I heard it on the grapevine.

He won't be hard to find. You can always pick him out of a bunch of people.

Guys like that really shirk my ass.

In certain backward countries, people can't even read. They're illegitimate.
Marriage makes you smarter?

They were speaking in a foreign language. I'm not bilateral, so I didn't understand them.

You never know what might happen, but don't hold your hopes up.
Then I won't get my breath, either.

When we visited Italy last year, we went to the museum that has the original painting of "The First Supper."
I heard there's a whole series.

Don't give me that crap. It's not my first day on the block, you know.

Boy you really hit the ball right on the nose.

You can't beat that with a rock.
Try a stick.

Some stores are open 24 by 7.

You don't have to be a brain scientist to figure that one out.

I left it on the table. Maybe it grew legs and flew away.

My boss is always breathing down my throat.
If mine did that, I'd have to hit him.

I just can't think of it but it's right on the tip
of my head.

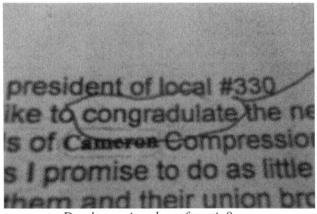

Don't you just love fanetix?

I don't know about you, but I would do that
without a heartbeat.
Wow! I don't believe I could.

I really get a load out of people like that.

Man, that guy was really something, all cool,
calm, and collective.

I don't need sunglasses. I have bifocals. When
I go outside, they darken automatically.

My mother in law and her daughter have been fighting for years. It's an oncoming thing. *Get out of the way!*

He doesn't look it but that guy's a little long in the mouth.

I don't want to discuss it any more. It's a mute point. *I didn't hear it, anyway.*

Small things come in good packages. *Is that another thing that everybody but me knows?*

I watched that novel on TV last night.

Life is a bundle of shit. Then you die and pay some more. *Words of wisdom.*

Be careful when he's around. That guy is like an elephant in a china shop. *Whatever you do, keep him away from the cabinet.*

Tonight's going to be special. I can tell. There is a certain aviance in the room.

Have a seat right here and let me put your thoughts to ease.

A man's got to do what a man does.

I bought a new pressure washer. It's got 20,000 B.T.U.s of pressure.

We'll document everything that happens. I'm sure we can find something that we can use to set a premise.

See that brown stain on his fingertips? That's a tell tell sign that he's a smoker.

I know a sure fire cure for a hangover. You just gotta do what bit you the night before.

It was a waste of time showing the house to them. They wanted it for a song and dance.
At least they didn't try to buy it for a song.

I hate when people drive with their bright lights on. That really ticks my cookie off.

I'm sure there are many different chains of thought on that subject.

You've been a lazy bum for two years. I think it's time for you to step up to the pump.

Those kids were very fortunate to have had the best of every world.
There are more than two?

Look at that crowd. I wonder what all the hubba-dub is about.
Maybe someone dropped a bombshell.

Work is funny. Sometimes we're busy and sometimes we're not. We seem to go in spirits.

Well, you know what they say. Honesty is the best.
Isn't it though?

On what planet?

If you want to make a good impression, make sure to put your best face forward.

No, I don't know what will happen in a couple weeks. It's not like I have a silver ball I can look into.

Johnny was like that as a kid too. He always played outside of the lines.

My boss was really on my throat today.
At least he wasn't breathing down it.

Once, when I was a kid, my mother caught me stealing. I'll never die to forget that one.

I was just sitting there, watching the TV, when it happened. I had one of those ha-ha moments.
Ah. I just had one too!

When I hit that car, my windbag was instantly deployed.
I wish mine would get deployed.

When people have sex with animals, it's called Beastiology.
I think that's the study of sex with animals.

I really felt that pit in my stomach.

I swear, they're just like a couple old hens…always haggling.
Over what?

We went to the casino last night. I lost forty dollars but I'm still ahead of the ball game. *Stop gambling. You don't want to end up living in the ball park.*

I went off the beaten track.

I really loved Zero Mostel in, "Fiddler on a Hot Tin Roof."

I always seem to get in the way, like a bad penny.

My ex-wife used to gamble like a fish.

I haven't seen my boss all morning. Something must be amok.

To hear him tell it, he's done it all. I bet he helped raise the flag at Hirojima. *I think you mean Iwo Shima.*

My in-laws go through food like shit through a tin horn.

Those kinds of people will never get it. It's beyond their realm.

The wind was blowing like a freight train, last night.

That new restaurant is supposed to have excellent fillet min yawn.

Maybe if he got in trouble, it might put a light under him.

It was as if the snowball from hell descended upon us.
Not a chance.

It's not exactly rocket surgery.
Or brain science.

Some people don't even have twenty cents to rub together.
Some don't have two minutes either.

I'd better be careful what I say or they'll be hauling my ass out of here in a rubber truck.

You'll never find him now. You'd have better luck taking a shot in a haystack.

Leaves lose their color in the fall from lack of chloroform.

It takes all kinds to make a village.

Everyone should learn how to do the Heineken Maneuver.
I do it every weekend.

Humans differ from most other animals because we have disposable thumbs.

My bank sent me an insignificant funds notice.
Maybe you should put more money in your account.

I've been having a hard time putting on my boots lately. I guess I'm not as ambidextrous as I used to be.

That thought will forever be in the front of my mind.
Better than being engraved in your head.

Those guys did everything under the book.
Good thing it wasn't everything in the sun.

You can't expect me to know all that stuff. I'm not a brain wizard, you know.
Or a rocket surgeon, I'll bet.

I don't know how to correctly promounce that word.
No kidding.

For every two weeks we work, we can accure one half a vacation day.

You can't just throw all that stuff into a box.
You have to be a little preciseful.

That was like a bundle in a haystack.
Take a shot at it.

My sister has to do everything in her own
weird way. I think she has excessive,
compulsive disorder.

That old-fashioned diner makes drinks from
scratch. Apple, watermelon, whatever you
want. They'll make any contraption you could
think of.

If you shop at a bigger store, they should have
more of the majority of things.

Last week my boss left early. You should
have seen all the guys milking the clock.
Did they get anything?

Your corporation is greatly appreciated.
*Maybe they should appreciate the workers
too.*

I was so quiet you could hear a pen drop.

They bought that property for pennies on the
acre.

Don't worry. Those guys will stick around.
They know where they get their bread
buttered.

You can't keep hiring inexperienced help.
They will always be a sore thumb in our
asses.
Might make their thumbs feel better.

Now we'll have to do this job another way.
We have no other recoil.

I don't get too involved in the small jobs at
work, because when a bigger one comes
along it always takes presidents.

I hate it when my mother in law visits. She
just crams my lifestyle.

Everything was going just fine till you came
along and rained on my cheerios.

I just want you to know that I'm here for your
disposal.
Don't get rid of me too quickly, though.

I'm very lucky, lately. I must have an
elephant on my shoulder.
Did you find him in a china shop?

I have a wish list too.

He married a girl who was way too young for him. He's such a grave robber.

My sister helps me plant my garden every year. She's the one with the thumb.
I guess hers wasn't disposable.

Ad in the local paper. For Sale: John Deere Utility Tractor with Excessories.
So, are there too many, or are they too big for the tractor?

When it comes to money, some people just can't resist themselves.
Kind of narcissistic, isn't it?

There was a gang of thugs, reaping havoc across the countryside.
I guess you do reap what you sow.

It was the better of two evils.

Everyone knows that revenge is sweeter when it's cold.
I'm starting to think I'm quite uninformed.

That woman's as crazy as the day goes by.

Whenever I go to Canada, my cell phone automatically goes into roving mode.
Keep it in your pocket. It won't go anywhere.

Last night, I opened the curtains just in time to see a large moth flirt by.
I think she noticed you, too.

I had to work down in the ditch today. I guess I drew the low straw.

I saw him out of the side of my head.

It's about time for you to step up to the platter.

Well, I wouldn't know the answer to that just
off the back of my head.
What about the side of it?

I don't know how you remember all that stuff.
You must have a steel trap.

He's kind of a lee asian between the bank and
its customers.

Most bourbons come from the same refinery.

It's all just water under the dam.

You know how it is around here. The one
hand doesn't talk to the other.

Guess I was wrong. Looks like I'll be the one
swallowing craw.

That room was so crowded, it'll be a
masterpiece trying to get out of there.

I got that bike put together without any
directions. I was just free winging it.

I don't understand any of that. It's all Italian
to me.

I'm as American as cherry pie.

That job is so easy it's a no minder.
I'm sure you can handle it.

I guess they'll just have to learn to turn their cheeks.

Look at the window. It's Jack Frost nipping at your toes.

Then why is it on selve 7?

I knew they were lying all along. It was just a rouge.

She didn't even beat an eye.

If the Buffalo Bills win this game, a lot of fans will have sugarplums dancing in their heads.

I've had a pit in my stomach all week.
You should eat something.

The bleeding was so bad, the doctor had to quarterize him.

Sometimes you just have to take the bull by the reigns.
I'll take the reigns over the horns any day.

Q: Are you sure about that?
A: Yes. I would swear a hundred dollars.

Around here, rumors spread like wildflower.

It's the perfect kind of nightclub where music lovers could conglomerate.

I don't have excess to that information.

Those people were having illusions of grandeur.

That place has the best fillet Ming yung.
I didn't know that was a Chinese dish.

I know her phone number like a heartbeat.

People heard about his exploits for miles on end.
I could listen for hours around.

Sometimes you got to take the punches as they roll.

Your reputation supersedes you.

You can't trust any lawyers. They're all from the same school of science.

I think he truly inspires to be just like his brother.

I really hate having discussions with him. We just end up arguing schematics.
My wife and I do the same thing with blueprints.

When it rains, it falls.

I did it first thing this morning. Right out of the bat.

Sometimes it comes to push and shove.
I hate when that happens.

I just happened to draw the short end.
At least it wasn't the low straw.

If that's not available, I'll have to fandangle something.

You took it right out of my breath.

It was up toward the beginning of the story. Right around the middle.

I worked on my book for a few years in January.
Good for you, Bob.

After the last setback, interest in the project seems to be weaning.
It's about time you started working on your own project.

They threw a very nice party for me. They went the whole seven yards.
If they were a little smarter, they could have gone the extra two.

You want a fight, do you? Well, you better be ready 'cause the chains are off.

There are lots of poor people living in absolute squander.
Should have been more careful with their money.

I thought my keys were in my purse but they weren't. Now I'm really S.O.S.

I sure showed him. He just put his head between his tail and walked away.

The delivery man asked me to put my John Deere on the line.

There was an article in the paper about South Carolina wanting to recede from the rest of the country.

After ten games, we finally lost one and broke our winning string.

His whole family was there to see his performance. He must have been in his pride.

Those guys were a little slow at the switch. *Those guys, again?*

When it comes to cooking, my wife loves to experiment, but sometimes she goes out of hand.

If only it was one size biger.

The shop where I work has three shifts. We're open 24/7, 375 days a year.

Don't believe those commercials. They're sending us sublibial messages.

I believe the scientists were right. It does seem like we're experiencing global warning.

Don't go putting the horse before the barn.

He took my sails right out of the wind.

Why people default on their student loans:
1. My professor never returned the photographs I gave him.
2. I really didn't get anything out of that class.
3. That guy was a lousy teacher.

It's really hard to work with someone breathing over your neck.
Especially when you have to stand up.

A. "This call is an attempt to collect a debt. You have a defaulted student loan."
B. "I can't pay it."
A. "But you're employed. Surely you must get a paycheck."
B. "I'm a yoga instructor. Can I come there and teach yoga in lieu of payment?"
A. "No, you can't."
B. "Can you ask?"
A. "No, we don't do that."
B. "But, can you just ask?"
A. "Sure." (hangs up)

I lost my debit card so I called my bank to put a halt on it.

I'll sell it to you for fifty bucks. Cash on the barrelhead.

That woman just exerts confidence.
Sounds difficult.

You shouldn't say things about other people, unless you live in a glass house. Then you can cast the first stone.

He was as calm as a cucumber.
That's cool.

My son failed fourth grade. Make your kids study so they don't suffer the same feat.

Everything was fine until Jack showed up.
That took me right out of the element.

Joe's boss put him right on the carpet this morning.
I would have quit when he breathed down my throat.

Sometimes, I always do that.

Last night I practiced playing one-string chords.

Well, that one really tops the cake.

Kids today have no work ethnic.

That guy must have been a cycle path.
Why, was someone riding him?

Some days, I don't get up until the crack of noon.

Those people were living in a pig style.

It's about time the state and county worked hand in glove, with each other.

Sure, he walks the walk, but can he speak the speak?

That restaurant is probably too small to acclimate a large crowd.

I like it and my wife doesn't. It's a point of attention.
And I'd bet she's got yours.

I didn't want to go but they were quite animate about it.
Were they waving their arms?

We tend to frown against that sort of thing.

All I know is, you don't want to be the guy that killed the golden goose.

Handicuffed people need a special parking area.

With more than 30 years of experience, he brings a good amount of hindsight to the job.
I'm surprised he lasted that long.

If he doesn't bring that back, I'll go after him like a thief in the night-just like Jesus did.

I bought it at the dollar store. It cost a dollar.
I kind of figured that.

I wouldn't have believed it but I saw it with my own mind.
You must have Mental Pelethany.

Don't be so hasty. You can't just do things at whim.

That's food for fodder.
I would think so.

My son doesn't have a very good work ethic, but I'm trying to install that in him.
Is your son a computer?

The sailor got in trouble again and was sent to the brink.
I'm sort of on the brink myself.

When you do a good deed, it usually comes
back to you multiple-fold.
Is that more or less than tenfold.

This world is going to hell in a handcart.

You're only scratching the tip of the iceberg.

Today, we learned that America is the
smelting pot of the world.

Whenever we get something good, our
neighbors want to jump on the bang wagon.

Nowadays, kids rarely use the telephone.
They're either texting or talking on
spacebook.

My brother is amerdextrious.

I think I'm going over the deep edge.

All that doesn't amount to a hill of shit.

That mistake cast him a lot of squid.

Vice a versa.

You never want to bite a gift horse.
Especially in the mouth.

I have a second job at night. They pay me under the books.

The woods behind our house is overrun with fallow cats.
Maybe you should plant something there.

That's not the girl I saw but she buries a resemblance to her.

The out of control van careered across several lanes of traffic.

You know how it works here. You wash my back and I'll wash yours.
Just don't breathe down my throat.

I don't care. Half a dozen, one of the other.

The news reported that the rebels had amassed a rather large cachet of weapons.
That must have smelled nice.

My arm still hurts from yesterday. I banged my tickle bone.

He keeps turning up like an old penny.
As long as he doesn't get in the way.

I think it's about time we put this rest to bed.

That poor dog. He sure looks like he's at a loss for words.

The woman next door is a widower.
How did that happen?

That was the first thing that came to my head.

All we were looking for was that lining in a bottle.

My father always told us, "Keep your eyes open and your nose to the ground."

That is the sixty-four dollar question.

I'll just toss a coin in the air and see what happens.
It can only land heads or tails.

Last week, we went to a party way out in the boondoggles.

That's a lot to pay for that pound of flesh.
A pound of flesh is never cheap.

They had better be on the lookout. I'm going after them and I'm fixin' for bear.

As long as I've known him, he's had a short trigger.

My buddy, John, is a real straight edge.

Hey, Friday the thirteenth is on a Friday this month.

It's pretty good, but it's not the end all to end all.

She's always been a thorn in my ass.

He came at me with a full head of speed.

I'll never babysit those kids again. They had me at the wit end.

I'm telling you, I was so scared I almost shit a green brick.
Was that on St. Patrick's Day?

I had his picture in my face, but I couldn't get to it.
Open your eyes.

You can't eat the banana until you put off the peel.
You can only put things off for so long.

I was looking through my change the other day, and found a 1909 DVD penny.

My wife's favorite drink is Champagne and orange juice. It's called a Formosa.

It was during the mid 1800's that the Indians uprised.

They wanted the whole shittin' caboodle.

I've been down that route before.

You can send me e-mail or contact me viva Facebook.

Ontario is the largest providence of Canada.

I don't think my boss fully appreciates that I worked my ass on that project.
That's probably why he doesn't appreciate it.

I could tell that he was lying in his teeth.

He only got that job because his father pulled some chains.

My brother had a few accommodations from the Marine Corps.
Well, you can't be expected to serve without someplace to stay.

My grandparents have a little cabin off on the beaten path.

I have a suspicion that this deal isn't going to happen. I'm just waiting for the shoe to fall.

You can figure it out. Just try to use deductible reasoning.
How long do you think that'll last?

They pulled just about every trick in the bag.

He stole that right in front of your nose.
Good thing it wasn't from under your face.

This company can't seem to do anything right. They're forever shooting themselves in the arm.
You hit it right on the nail.

You're always crying about your bad luck. Let's break out the flutes.

I have a couple garnishes on my paycheck.
What did I tell you about keeping that off the table?

I took some cold medicine about an hour ago. Boy, I feel a hundred bucks.

Was it ever busy at work, today. We were all running around with our heads cut off.
No wonder it was busy.

No need to handle them with kit gloves. They won't break.

No wonder those kids are brats. Their parents buy them everything under the moon.
Maybe they should be in bed a little earlier.

It's just another case of the pot calling the kettle fat.
He needs to stop doing that.

We could keep going but nobody wants to beat a dead moose.
Or a bush, for that matter.

Let's get him down here. We'll see if he can walk the talk.
I'd like to see him talk the walk.

Who cares if he takes all the credit? Some people just feel the need to feed their alter egos.

They'll get theirs soon enough. I'll buy my time for now.

I usually don't plan my weekends. Everything is just off the cuff.

I'm still trying to grasp my mind over that.

Send me an e-mail and carbon the other supervisors.

That pitch dissected home plate.

I don't know why they opened that box. Nobody authored them to do that.

When are we going to have our big sheding?

Time is in essence.

He is in good health due to a regiment of exercise and eating right.

That guy is always talking out of the side of his neck.
Can he see out of the side of his head too?

I wouldn't vote for him. He was swinging from the fence on a few issues.

I just took a stab in the dark.

I can't find my wallet. Would you please keep your eyes out?

Gentlemen, start your onions.

You better watch yourself from now on.
You're walking on thin ground.

Don't say anything around him. He always
has to put his two pieces in.

The boat was finally moving after catching a
nice wind tail.

He's not the smartest bulb in the box.
Probably only a 20 watter.

I did a killing in the market last year.
And you're telling people?

Guys like him are always shaking the boat.

Always put your best self forward.
Why stop at a foot?

My boss has a hard time making decisions.
He's always hem hogging.

He has his job down to a system.

I graduated college Beta Kappa.

Never kick a gift horse in the mouth.
Not until you've looked in it first.

They really dragged their heels on this one.

When his boss retires, John will become his
protégé.
John is retiring?

That guy is too smart for his britches.
Too big for his own good, too.

When the guy on top does the wrong thing, it
hurts everyone below him. That's called the
accordion effect.
*Is that why it's so annoying when guys play
dominos badly?*

Don't get mad. He's only busting your chain.

Sounds to me like someone woke up on the wrong end of the tweezers.
I'd be pretty cranky too.

This country is going to hell in a breadbasket.
It's roomier than a hand basket.

There are no simularities between the two pieces.

Twelve O'clock is the witching number.

When the shit hits the fan, I've learned how to pick myself up and make lemonade out of it.

They went down in a flame of glory.

Sometimes people can't help talking through their mouths.
Only sometimes?

You're really crossing a grey line there, aren't you?

He's a happy guy, from the top of his head to the bottom of his toes.

It was a good opportunity to get in on the bottom floor.

In our town we have churches of many
different dominations.
I like to make my own choices.

Did you hear his speech? He was really on top
of the ball.
*Would have been easier if he'd stayed on his
orange crate.*

We had to go to the airport and take our car
back to the rental returnal.

Sorry, I was just talking out loud.
Well, do it silently next time.

Don't ever forget, you get paid for what you
play.

After her mother died, Jane really went off the
deep side.

I guess you'll just have to take that with a bag
of salt.
Must really be awful.

That girl was really off the brand wall.

Most movie stars are quite used to being
hounded by the pavarotsie.
Singers too, I'll bet.

Stock prices went down steadily for two weeks, then, they rebounded and went right off the hook.

Beyond a doubt, everything I know was learned at home.

I can't believe my husband did that, even though it was against my better wishes.

My boss was all over me like flies on rice.
White rice?

A new girl started at work today. She's from Ukrania.

Everyone knows you get more bees with honey.
Not everyone.

The scientific name for your jawbone is the Malibu.

Those guys never take responsibility for anything. They only know how to pass the hat.
Is that where the buck is?

The best thing for a stuffy nose is a pseudomenaphine.

Don't say anything to him. You'll just be adding to the fuel.

My wife woke up all wide-eyed and bushy tailed.

It was the worst thing to ever come off the face of the Earth.

My favorite dessert is Pie ala load.

I'll get a head start and meet you at the agreed upon coordinations.

While vacationing in the Bahamas, we went for a ride on a bottomless boat.
Really!

You drilled your own bed. Now you have to lie in it.

My wife is so emotional. She cries at the drop of a pin.
Then don't drop any.

We went to see a new band last night. They play bluesgrass.

I finally called the doctor. Now I'll be sitting on hot irons until he calls back.
Hope he calls soon.

Our new porch light is action motivated.
We all need some motivation.

He had done that type of work before so he
denoted it on his application.

Saturday night we are going to the big shing
ding.

About the Author

Jimmy Neureuther lives in Chaffee, NY with his wife, Valerie, and a blind cat named Bella. He is a member of the writers group Basics to Bylines. This is his first published work and he is currently collecting entries for his second installment called, *This is my Piece of the Resistance.*

Acknowledgments

First and foremost, I'd like to thank my wife Valerie for putting up with my lack of doing things around the house. (She's not used to that?)

John Yea, Joe Kowalerowski, Joe Cox, for tirelessly feeding me things they heard.

Jeffrey Mikulski for patiently waiting to resume our musicality. Very soon Brother.

Mike Neureuther, Valerie, Kristen, Bruce and anyone else who has given me the occasional tidbit.

Edie Koch, for all your time and knowledge. If this is good, it's because of you.

30429141R00054

Made in the USA
Charleston, SC
15 June 2014